FACT-O-PEDIA

DINOSAURS AND BIRDS

MOONSTONE

Published in Moonstone
by Rupa Publications India Pvt. Ltd 2023
7/16, Ansari Road, Daryaganj
New Delhi 110002

Sales centres:
Prayagraj Bengaluru Chennai
Hyderabad Jaipur Kathmandu
Kolkata Mumbai

Copyright © Rupa Publications India Pvt. Ltd 2023

All rights reserved.
No part of this publication may be reproduced, transmitted,
or stored in a retrieval system, in any form or by any means,
electronic, mechanical, photocopying, recording or otherwise,
without the prior permission of the publisher.

P-ISBN: 978-93-5702-296-5
E-ISBN: 978-93-5702-290-3

First impression 2023

10 9 8 7 6 5 4 3 2 1

This book is sold subject to the condition that it shall not,
by way of trade or otherwise, be lent, resold, hired out, or otherwise
circulated, without the publisher's prior consent, in any form of binding
or cover other than that in which it is published.

Contents

Introduction	6
Rise of Dinosaurs	8
Age of Reptiles	10
Discovering Dinosaurs	12
Classification	14
Shapes and Sizes	16
Fastest and Slowest	18
Lifespan and Reproduction	20
Tyrannosaurus Rex	22
Spinosaurus	24
Ankylosaurus	26
Stegosaurus	28
Diplodocus	30
Apatosaurus	32
Velociraptor	34
Deinonychus	36
Dilophosaurus	38
Baryonyx	40
Extinction of Dinosaurs	42
Glossary	44
Answers	46
Introduction	48
Evolution of Birds	50
Feathers	52

Bird Beaks and Feeding	54
Mating	56
Nests	58
Young Ones	60
Migration	62
Flightless Birds	64
Game Birds	66
Seabirds	68
Swimming Birds	70
Birds of Prey	72
Forest Birds	74
Perching Birds	76
Freshwater Birds	78
Nocturnal Birds	80
Hummingbirds	82
Intelligence	84
Glossary	86
Answers	88

DINOSAURS

Introduction

Dinosaurs were very fascinating animals. They appeared 228 million years ago and dominated the earth for about 160 million years. Dinosaurs were reptiles and, like all reptiles, they had a backbone, scaly skin and hatched from eggs. The word 'dinosaur' was derived from the Greek words *deinos*, meaning 'terrible', and *sauros*, meaning 'lizard'. Hence, dinosaur means 'terrible lizard' but neither were dinosaurs lizards nor were all of them terrible.

Dinosaurs came in various shapes and sizes. Some dinosaurs such as *compsognathus* were as small as chickens while some were as big as skyscrapers such as sauropods. The existence of these different dinosaurs was revealed by their fossil remains, and there's still a lot to discover about these mighty animals.

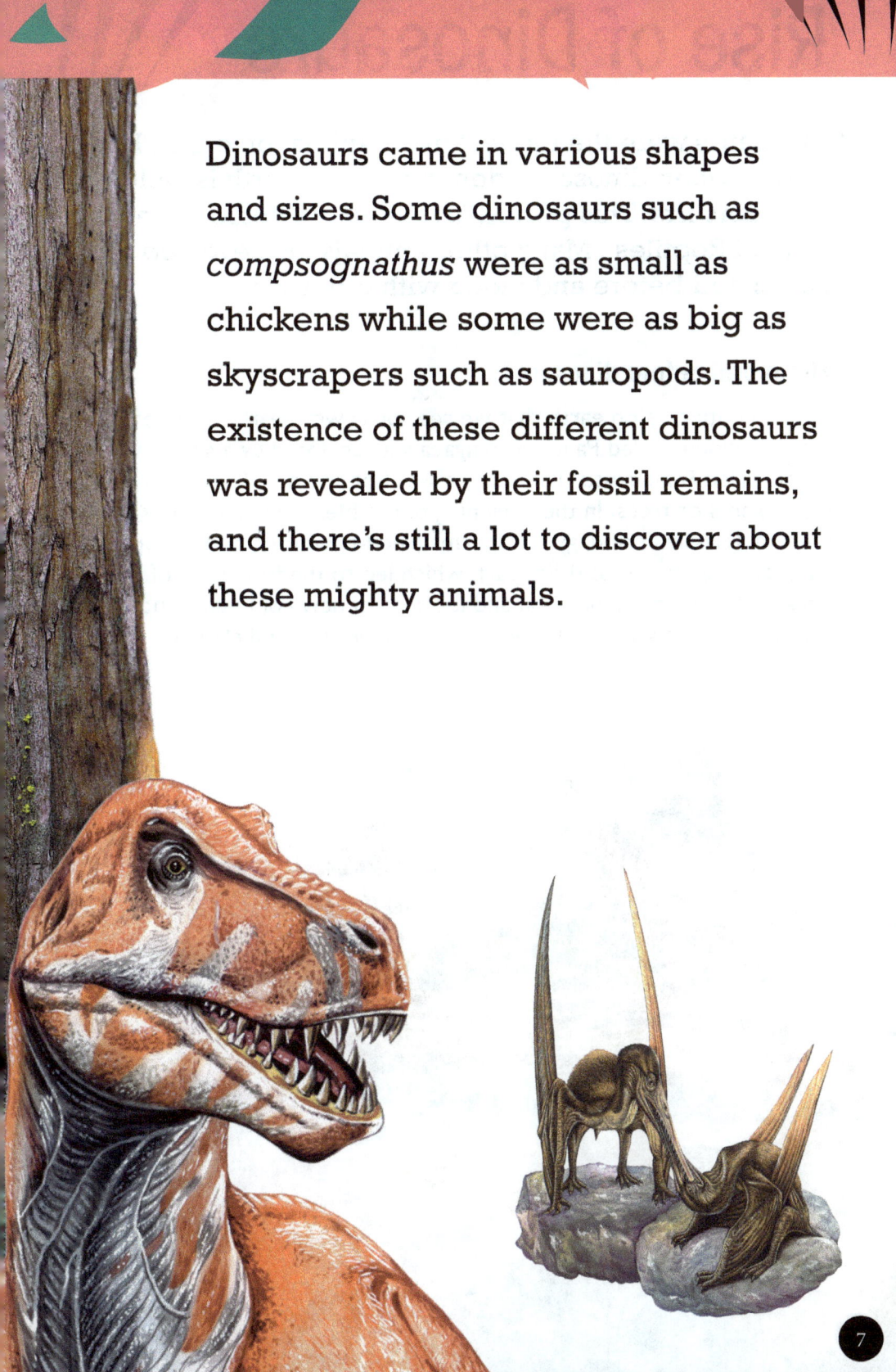

Rise of Dinosaurs

Dinosaurs were the longest lived animal on earth. The period when dinosaurs dominated the earth is called the Mesozoic Era. This period is famously referred to as the 'Age of Reptiles'. Many other animals also evolved and flourished before and along with dinosaurs.

The world before dinosaurs

All the continents on earth that we see today were earlier part of a big supercontinent called Pangaea. Pangaea was enclosed by a single world ocean called *Panthalassa*. The climate was hot and dry. There were not many plants or trees. In the beginning of the Mesozoic Era, that is, during the late Triassic Period, gymnosperms (seed-producing plants) appeared. Pangaea also started to drift apart, which led to the formation of new oceans. The changing position and location of new continents and oceans brought about a gradual change in the temperature and climate.

Evolution of dinosaurs

Dinosaurs evolved from the family of primitive reptiles known as *Archosaurs* (ruling lizards). They led to the evolution of *Pterosaurs*, Saurischians, Ornithischians and Theocondonts. Archosaurs were therapsids, were quadruple and much smaller than dinosaurs. Their splay-footed postures were one of the several characteristics that set them apart from their more legendary successors. During the late Triassic Period, the earliest dinosaurs appeared. They were small in size, bipedal and meat-eaters.

Other animals

Many animals such as pelycosaurs, amphibians such as ichthyostegas and diplocaulus, therapsids and anapsids were living before the arrival of dinosaurs. Mesosaurs were anapsids and looked like the present-day alligators, with sharp needle-like teeth and strong jaws. Pelycosaurs were in great abundance, with Dimetrodon being one of the most well-known. It was a large reptile and had a sail on its back, most probably for regulating its body temperature. Cynognathus, a therapsid, was about the size of a large dog and dominated the land. Apart from all these animals, giant dragonflies, wasps and sawflies also lived before and among dinosaurs.

Facts
- The earliest dinosaurs were merely 1-2 m long.
- Herrerasaurus was one of the earliest dinosaurs that lived around 230 million years ago.

The era when dinosaurs dominated the earth is called _____.

Age of Reptiles

The Mesozoic Era lasted from 251–65 million years ago on a geological timescale and is divided into three periods—Triassic, Jurassic and Cretaceous. These periods are further divided into many epochs and ages. During this era, the temperature was warmer. Apart from the evolution of dinosaurs, many types of plants, such as ferns, cycads, ginkgos, gymnosperms and angiosperms appeared and began to diversify.

Triassic Period (251–199.6 million years ago)

The earliest forms of dinosaurs appeared during the Triassic Period, which were fairly small, lightweight and agile. *Herrerasaurus* and Eoraptors were some of the earliest bipedal meat-eating dinosaurs. No one knew that these little dinosaurs would rule the land. Many other reptiles such as therapsids, primitive crocodiles, flying reptiles such as pterosaurs and sea creatures such as ichthyosaurs evolved during this period. The climate in the Triassic Period was hot and dry.

▲ *Herrerasaurus*

Facts

- The first flowering plants, grasshoppers, ants, termites and aphids appeared during the late Cretaceous Period.
- French geologist and mineralogist Alexandre Brongniart named the Jurassic Period in the 19th century.

Jurassic Period (199.6–145.5 million years ago)

During this period dinosaurs flourished and became the largest land-dwelling animals. Giant herbivore sauropods like *Apatosaurus* and *Brachiosaurus* and smaller but fierce carnivore dinosaurs such as *Allosaurus* roamed the earth. *Archaeopteryx*, the earliest bird, also flew in the late Jurassic Period and probably evolved from the coelurosaurian dinosaur. During this time Pangaea split up into Laurasia and Gondwana, and the Panthalassa Ocean flooded the spaces between the continents and gave rise to new oceans. The climate became humid, which led to an increase in vegetation.

◀ *Apatosaurus*

Cretaceous Period (145.5–65.5 million years ago)

The Cretaceous Period marked the rise of different forms of dinosaurs. Heavily armoured dinosaurs like *Ankylosaurus*, *Triceratops* and Hylaeosaurus evolved along with beaked plant-eating ceratopsians and dome-headed pachycepalosaurs. *Pelecanimimus* was another unique dinosaur that had about 220 teeth, more than any other known dinosaur. The most terrifying predators of their time, such as T. rex, *Gigantosaurus,* and *Spinosaurus,* also lived during this period.

Triceratops ▶

Pterosaurs were flying reptiles. True/False?

Discovering Dinosaurs

We know about dinosaurs because of the fossils they left behind. Fossils are the remains or traces of plants and animals from the past. They are formed when an organism dies and its body gets buried in sand or mud. Over a period of time, the bones decay and are replaced by minerals provided the conditions are suitable. These minerals harden to become fossils. Dinosaur fossils have been found in the rock strata of every continent.

Dinosaur fossils

Dinosaur fossils can be divided into two main types: body fossils and trace fossils. Body fossils include bones, claws, teeth, skin and eggs and embryos, which tell us about the shape and size of dinosaurs. On the other hand, trace fossils include footprints, tracks, trails and burrows, which tell us about the behaviour and movements of dinosaurs.

◄ *The footprint fossil of a dinosaur*

Facts

- Megalosaurus was the first dinosaur to be discovered by William Buckland.
- Iguanodon was the first dinosaur to be identified and named by Gideon Mantell.

Fossil diggers

Fossil diggers are people who search fossils and examine them. They collect fossils, study them and determine their nature and behaviour. Since fossils are remains of ancient life, fossil diggers also find out the time and environment a fossil belongs to. They use chisels, drills and hammers to excavate fossils buried inside the earth. Fossil diggers are also called paleontologists, and the study of fossils is called paleontology. Some of the most famous paleontologists are Othniel C. Marsh, William Buckland, Gideon Mantell, Barnum Brown and Edward Drinker Cope. The word 'dinosaur', was coined in 1841 by Sir Richard Owen, an English paleontologist.

Aurornis xu: a recent fossil

What is the study of fossils called?

Recently scientists dug up a complete fossilized skeleton of a flying dinosaur in China. It is estimated that this dinosaur, named Aurornis xui, lived 150 million years ago and was the size of a modern-day chicken. It had very small, triangular teeth and its entire body was covered with primitive feathers. Aurornis xui is believed to be a close relative of *Archaeopteryx*.

Classification

All dinosaurs are broadly classified into two orders according to the structure of their pelvic bones and joints: saurischians or lizard-hipped dinosaurs and ornithischians or bird-hipped dinosaurs. In 1887, British paleontologist Harry Seeley divided dinosaurs into these classes.

Lizard-hipped dinosaurs

Lizard-hipped dinosaurs or saurischians were dinosaurs that had hip bones like that of lizards. Saurischians could walk using all their limbs. They were both herbivores and carnivores. They were also the first dinosaurs to evolve and dominated the land till the end of the Age of Reptiles. They are also believed to be the ancestors of birds. Saurischians are divided into two main groups: sauropods and theropods.

> Name the paleontologist who divided the dinosaurs into the groups saurischians and ornithischians.

▼ Compsognathus

Sauropods and theropods

All sauropods had an extremely long neck, a small head, tail, bulky body and walked on their four massive, pillar-like legs. They were the largest animals that ever walked on earth. *Diplodocus* and *Apatosaurus* were sauropods. On the other hand, theropods include both small and large carnivore dinosaurs. They were bipedal and had sharp teeth, curved claws on each of the forelimbs and hind limbs, and a stiff tail. *Gigantosaurus,* T. rex, *Compsognathus* and *Coelophysis* were some of the smallest theropods.

Bird-hipped dinosaurs

Bird-hipped dinosaurs or ornithischians had hip bone wider than that of saurischians. The pubis bone pointed downwards and towards the tail. They were bipedal as well as quadrupedal. Most ornithischians were duck-billed and armoured. They had bony plates on their back, while others had horns. Their skulls also had a small hole between the eye sockets and the nostrils. Ornithischians had a horny beak. They were plant-eaters, and their beak helped them to chew plants. Ornithopods, ankylosaurs, stegosaurs, ceratopsians and pachycephalosaurs were ornithischians.

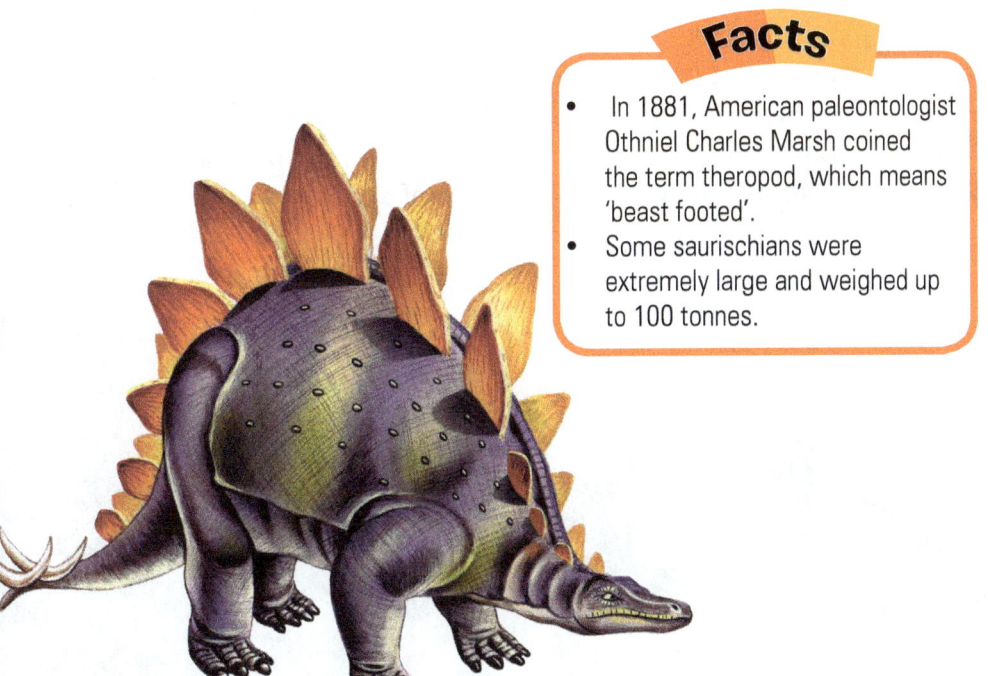

Facts

- In 1881, American paleontologist Othniel Charles Marsh coined the term theropod, which means 'beast footed'.
- Some saurischians were extremely large and weighed up to 100 tonnes.

Shapes and Sizes

Dinosaurs had varied shapes and sizes. Some were large, almost reaching the treetops while some were small, only about the size of a chicken. **Compsognathus**, **Microraptor** and **Mononykus** were some of the smallest dinosaurs that looked puny in front of the giants of their age—the sauropods.

Argentinosaurus

Argentinosaurus lived in South America about 97 to 94 million years ago, during the Cretaceous Period. It was the second biggest and heaviest dinosaur after the gigantic *Amphicoelias fragillimus*. Argentinosaurus was about 37 m long when measured from head to tail, 12 m tall and weighed up to 100 tonnes. It laid eggs about the size of a rugby ball.

Compsognathus

Compsognathus was about the size of a chicken. It was one of the smallest lizard-hipped theropods. It lived during the late Jurassic Period about 156 to 145 million years ago. *Compsognathus* was 1m long and weighed about 3.5 kg. It was a swift runner and its speed was its only defence against predators.

Microraptor

Microraptor was one of the smallest bird-like dinosaurs. It was a four-winged dinosaur that had well-developed feathers. It lived about 130 million years ago, during the Cretaceous Period. *Microraptor* was about 40–101 cm long and weighed up to 1 kg. It spent most of its time on trees and might have flown from one tree to another in search of food.

Argentinosaurus lived during the _____.

Facts

- *Amphicoelias fragillimus,* the largest and heaviest of all dinosaurs, was about 40–60 m long and weighed up to 135 tonnes.
- The feathers covering the hind and forelimbs of *Microraptor* were true flight feathers as that of modern birds.

▼ *Compsognathus*

Fastest and Slowest

Some dinosaurs were small, lightweight and lean, while some were huge, heavyweight and plump. They walked and ran at different speeds according to their shapes and sizes. Some dinosaurs could run as fast as ostriches, while some plodded slowly like elephants. Sauropods were the slowest of all dinosaurs, and ornithomimids were probably the fastest dinosaurs.

Muttaburrasaurus

Muttaburrasaurus walked the earth about 100 million years ago during the Cretaceous Period. It was about 9 m long when measured from snout to tail, 5 m tall and weighed about 4 tonnes. *Muttaburrasaurus* could walk on its hind limbs as well as on all limbs. Like human beings, it could walk around 4–5 km per hour. It could also run up to 15 km per hour.

▲ *Muttaburrasaurus*

Struthiomimus

Struthiomimus was a fast-running omnivorous dinosaur. It was about 4 m long, 1.2 m tall, and weighed about 149.6 km. It lived about 75 million years ago in North America. *Struthiomimus* also resembled the ostrich like its relative *Ornithomimus*. Its hind limbs were lean and long and it had large clawed feet like an ostrich's. It also had a beak-like mouth similar to that of an ostrich. This is why *Struthiomimus* was called an ostrich dinosaur. It could run at a speed of more than 64 km per hour.

▼ *Struthiomimus*

Coelphysis

Coelphysis was one of the earliest dinosaurs. It lived during the late Triassic Period, about 225 million years ago. It was 3 m long from nose to tail and had a long head, neck and tail. It also had three fingers and long sharp claws. *Coelphysis* had a pointed mouth and very sharp teeth. It could run as fast as 40 km per hour on its lean and sturdy legs. *Coelphysis* could also leap, trot, dart and jump with swift motions.

Ornithomimus

Ornithomimus walked the earth about 65 million years ago, during the late Cretaceous Period. It was a very agile, lightweight, bipedal dinosaur. It resembled an ostrich in many ways—it had long and lean legs built for speed. It also had a small and toothless beak-like mouth perfect for pecking food like an ostrich's. *Ornithomimus* was 3.6 m long from head to tail and weighed about 159 km. Its powerful leg muscles helped it run at a speed of 70 km per hour.

In which year was *Muttaburrasaurus* found?

Facts

- Muttaburrasaurus was named after a town in Australia, where it was discovered in 1963.
- It is only during the old age that Ornithomimus developed larger feathers on the arms that looked like wings. When young, it had down-like feathers.

Lifespan and Reproduction

The exact lifespan of dinosaurs is not known. However, according to some paleontologists, they lived about 70–300 years. The recent discovery of growth rings in fossilized dinosaur bones has given the paleontologists a new way to find out their lifespan. Giant sauropods are believed to have lived up to 100 years. Like all reptiles, dinosaurs reproduced by laying eggs.

Eggs

The first dinosaur egg shells were discovered in France in 1869, and till now dinosaur eggs and nests have been found at 199 sites around the world. Dinosaur eggs had varied shapes and sizes with hard and brittle shells. They contained an inner membrane (amnion) that provided moisture to the embryo. Female dinosaurs laid eggs either in circles or in straight lines. Sauropods laid round eggs almost as big as a basketball and did not care for their babies. Theropod eggs were elongated, whereas ornithopod eggs were fairly rounded and slightly elongated at one end while being thicker at the other.

Babies

According to some paleontologists, most newborn dinosaurs were too small and feeble to survive on their own. However, some could take care of themselves right after birth. Many dinosaurs cared for their babies and looked after them. Some dinosaurs like *Oviraptor* and *Maiasaura* also incubated their eggs. The name *Maiasaura* means 'the good Mother lizard'. It is called so because it fed its young ones with ferns and leaves and tended them until they were one or two years old.

Nests

Dinosaurs built nests by scraping out a wide bowl-shaped hole in the ground. They covered their nests with plants and sand to make a mound. The more complicated nests were rimmed with mud.

Facts

- A baby Diplodocus was about 1 m long and weighed about 30 kg.
- The eggs of a sauropod were the size of a football.

Where were the first dinosaur egg shells discovered?

Tyrannosaurus Rex

T. rex was the most fearsome predator that ever roamed the earth. It lived during the late Cretaceous Period about 65 million years ago. It ruled the land it inhabited and was one of the largest meat-eating dinosaurs to have lived on earth. Its name means the 'tyrant lizard king'.

What did it look like?

T. rex was about 12 m long, 4-6 m tall and weighed about 4535-6350 kg. It had very small arms that extended up to a length of 91 cm, and were of little use to the dinosaur. Each jaw of T.rex was 1.2 m long and had 50-60 long and serrated conical teeth. Each tooth was 30 cm long. Like most predators, T. rex had depth perception, which was characterized by its large brain and eyes. Its massive head was 1.5 m long and marked with big eyes. It had a scaly skin like a crocodile's.

How did it walk?

T. rex walked on its mighty hind legs. It had three toes on each foot and was capable of taking large strides. It was a fast runner but not as fast as other smaller theropods. Fossil footprints of T. rex suggest that it used to walk on its toes rather than on the whole feet.

Diet

T. rex was the most ferocious dinosaur. It hunted other dinosaurs and was also a scavenger. Its sharp sense of smell helped it find an already decaying animal. T. rex could eat up to 230 kg of food in one bite.

What does the name T. rex mean?

Facts

- T. rex's fossils were first uncovered in 1900 by Barnum Brown in Mongolia and North America.
- A recent report suggests that the healing properties of dinosaur skin were similar to those of a modern reptile's.

Spinosaurus

Spinosaurus was the biggest terrestrial meat-eater that ever walked on earth. It was a theropod that lived in northern Africa about 95 million years ago (late Cretaceous Period). T. rex and **Gigantosaurus** were relatives of **Spinosaurus** but the latter was more gigantic and terrifying than the former.

Special sail

Spinosaurus was famous for its long neural spine jutting out from its spinal column that could be as long as 1.8 m. This is why it was called *Spinosaurus* which means 'spined lizard'. The spine was covered with a thin skin and formed a sail-like structure. The sail movement helped *Spinosaurus* to maintain its body temperature. It could also be used for attracting mates.

Facts

- Spinosaurus could catch aquatic animals like fish with its crocodile-like mouth and teeth. It could hunt both on land and in water.
- Spinosaurus outweighed Gigantosaurus by 500 kg and T. rex by 1000 kg.

What did it look like?

Spinosaurus had a short but stiff tail and a long and narrow head similar to that of a crocodile. The head was about 2 m long, and its mouth was filled with many long and sharp non-serrated teeth. The teeth of the lower and upper jaws got interlocked like a zipper when it closed its mouth. *Spinosaurus* was about 15 m long when measured from nose to tail and 5 m tall. It weighed about 5443 kg and, unlike T. rex and *Gigantosaurus*, had larger forelimbs with four claws.

Sharp and brainy

Spinosaurus was a fierce hunter and had sharp depth perception. It was one of the few dinosaurs that were blessed with high brainpower. The intelligence of dinosaurs is calculated by their brain to body mass ratio.

> What does the name *Spinosaurus* mean?

Ankylosaurus

Ankylosaurus was a bird-hipped dinosaur that lived around 68–65 million years ago (Cretaceous Period). This phase marked the end of the Age of Reptiles. ***Ankylosaurus*** belonged to the family of armour-plated dinosaurs.

What did it look like?

Ankylosaurus was about 6 m to 9 m long, weighed about 4535 kg and walked quite slowly. Its hind legs were larger than its front legs; this helped the dinosaur to keep its belly off the ground, though its head stayed close to the ground. It used to graze on low-lying plants and, like all plant-eaters, it had a toothless beak. It had tiny leaf-shaped teeth that were located at the back of the jaws.

Fused lizard

The back, neck and tail of *Ankylosaurus* were covered in bony plates and spikes that looked like a turtle's carapace. *Ankylosaurus* is a Greek word that means 'fused lizard'. The dinosaur was named so since its bones and bony spikes were fused together along with the skin. The end of the tail also had a series of plates that were fused together. Its club-like tail was capable of delivering a powerful blow to predators. It had four spikes jutting out from the rear side of the head.

Facts

- Ankylosaurus tail club was nearly as large as its head.
- Paleontologists believe that Ankylosaurus was among the last dinosaurs to face extinction due to its ability to keep predators at bay and secure ample amount of food.

Ankylosaurus was a _____ hipped dinosaur.

Lookalike

Ankylosaurus closely resembled an animal called Doedicurus. Doedicurus was one of the species of the ancient animal, armadillo. The body of a Doedicurus was armoured with thick bony plates and spikes. It also had a spiked tail club. The only difference between the two was that Ankylosaurus was a dinosaur.

Stegosaurus

Stegosaurus inhabited the earth about 156–140 million years ago (late Jurassic Period). It was an armoured bird-hipped dinosaur. *Stegosaurus* lived in North America along with *Apatosaurus*, *Diplodocus*, *Allosaurus* and *Brachiosaurus*.

Family

Stegosaurus belonged to a family of armoured dinosaurs—stegosaurids. Stegosaurids had bony plates in a row alongside their back and tail. The bony plates are called thagomizer. *Kentrosaurus* and *Wuerhosaurus* are stegosaurids and had a similarly armoured body.

Plates on the back

Stegosaurus had 17 triangular, bony plates running along its back till the middle of its tail. The plates were filled with blood vessels and, according to paleontologists, helped the dinosaur to maintain its body temperature. The name *Stegosaurus* means 'roof lizard' and the dinosaur was named so because its plates were placed flat on its back like roof tiles. It also had two pairs of long, pointed plates (each being 1 m long) at the end of its tail.

▲ *Stegosaurus*

What did it look like?

Stegosaurus was 9 m long, around 3 m tall and weighed around 2000 kg. It had a small and narrow head, toothless beak-like mouth and small neck. *Stegosaurus* had a strong body and a sturdy tail that always remained far above the ground in an upward position. Its hind limbs were longer than its forelimbs, due to which its head remained close to the ground. *Stegosaurus* walked using all its limbs.

Facts

- Stegosaurus had a small brain that was almost the size of a walnut.
- Stegosaurus supplemented its diet by eating rocks known as gastroliths.

What does the name *Stegosaurus* mean?

Stegosaurus ▶

Diplodocus

Diplodocus was one of the largest lizard-hipped dinosaur that ever lived on earth. It lived about 150 million years ago (late Jurassic Period) in North America. **Diplodocus** belonged to the group of dinosaurs called sauropods. It lived in groups and migrated from one place to another in search of food.

What did it look like?

Diplodocus was one of the longest sauropods ever discovered. It was up to 30 m long when measured from head to tail. Its incredibly long neck measured around 8 m. *Diplodocus* weighed about 15 tonnes because of its hollow bones. It had a small head and bulky body that rested on its four strong legs. Its forelimbs were shorter than the hind limbs, and it had elephant-like massive claws with five toes and a thumb claw for defence.

> In which year was the first *Diplodocus* fossil found?

Long tail

Diplodocus had an extremely long tail. It was 14 m long and helped the dinosaur in balancing its long neck and body. The tail was thin towards the end and played a vital role in defence. *Diplodocus* could swish and crack its tail like a whip to scare away the enemies.

Diet

Diplodocus used its long neck for eating plant matter such as club mosses, ferns and horsetails from wetlands or forests where it could not enter. It spent much of its time munching leaves as its mouth was too small to eat a lot of food at a time. *Diplodocus* also swallowed little stones along with the food. The stones helped in grinding food in its stomach and thus aided in digestion.

Facts

- Diplodocus was also called the 'whip tail' dinosaur.
- Earl Douglass and Samuel W. Williston found the first Diplodocus fossil in 1877.

Apatosaurus

Apatosaurus walked the earth about 147–137 million years ago (Jurassic Period). It lived in what is now western North America. It was a sauropod and was quite similar to *Diplodocus* but was much stockier with a thicker neck and stronger pillar-like legs.

▲ *Apatosaurus*

What did it look like?

Apatosaurus had a small head, long neck and muscular body. Its mouth was filled with elongated pencil-like teeth in the front. *Apatosaurus* also had massive legs with elephant-like toes and a long tail. It kept its long tail off the ground when it walked and might have used it as a whip to ward off predators. It was up to 21 m long, 4.5 m tall and weighed around 36 tonnes. It had a very long whip-like tail.

Colossal cousins of Apatosaurus

Mamenchisaurus was one of Apatosaurus's cousin that was known for its extremely long neck. The neck was 14 m long, more than half of its body length, and had 19 vertebrae—the most among all dinosaurs. Amargasaurus, another cousin of Apatosaurus, lived during the early Cretaceous Period. It was not as large as the other sauropods but was a unique sauropod. Amargasaurus had a high backbone spine that resembled a horse-like mane. The spine ran from the back of its neck to the tail.

Apatosaurus vs Brontosaurus

Othniel Charles Marsh discovered the fossils of two dinosaurs and named them *Apatosaurus* and *Brontosaurus*. Nearly after a century, it was discovered that the two fossils were of the same dinosaur. *Brontosaurus* then came to be known as *Apatosaurus* as it was the first name assigned to the dinosaur by Marsh.

In which period did *Apatosaurus* live?

Facts

- Since Apatosaurus was so gigantic, it hardly had any predators.
- Apatosaurus used its long tail and the thumb claw on each leg as a weapon for crushing puny meat-eaters like Allosaurus.

Apatosaurus

Velociraptor

Velociraptor was a feathered lizard-hipped dinosaur that roamed the earth about 75 million years ago (Cretaceous Period). It belonged to the family of dromaeosaurids that had the largest brain among all dinosaurs and were very intelligent. Dromaeosaurs were small-sized, had a special killing claw and were very swift.

Mighty claws

Velociraptor had mighty sickle-shaped claws for killing prey. It also had a special killing claw on the second toe of each foot that was up to 10 cm long. *Velociraptor* lived and hunted in packs. It was a swift runner and could chase and kill larger dinosaurs like *Protoceratops* and Hadrosaurs easily. Its ability to run at great speeds and its mighty claws made it a formidable dinosaur on land.

What did it look like?

Velociraptor was about 1.8 m long, 60 cm tall and weighed up to 15 kg. It had a large head, pointed tail and longer hind limbs. It also had many serrated teeth, each being 3 cm long. It was a bipedal dinosaur and was very agile. It could run at a speed of 39 km per hour. The dinosaur had a fine feathery coat.

Velociraptor discovery

Velociraptor was first discovered in 1922 in the Gobi Desert, Mongolia, China. In 1924, American Museum of Natural History's President and Paleontologist, H.F. Osborn, described the fossil as *Velociraptor mongoliensis*. Another *Velociraptor* fossil was uncovered in a fighting position with a *Protoceratops* in 1971.

Resembling birds

Velociraptor shared many similarities with the modern birds. Like birds, it was bipedal and had hollow bones. According to some paleontologists, *Velociraptors* were warm-blooded like birds and had bird-like plumage. They also had strong arm and chest muscles.

▲ *Velociraptor*

Facts

- The name Velociraptor means 'speedy thief'. The dinosaur was named so because it was believed to steal the eggs of other dinosaurs.
- Velociraptor probably used its plumage to attract mates or for visual displays.

When and where was *Velociraptor* discovered?

Deinonychus

Deinonychus was a carnivorous dinosaur with long claws. It lived around 145.5 million to 99.6 million years ago (early Cretaceous Period). It belonged to the group of 'raptor' dinosaurs. It was a feathered lizard-hipped dinosaur and had a good sense of smell, sight and hearing.

What did it look like?

Deinonychus was a small lightweight dinosaur. It was about 2.5 m long, 1.5 m tall and weighed around 45 to 68 kg. It had an S-shaped neck and a slender tail. There were bony plates on its tail that made it stiff and helped the dinosaur to balance its body while running. This bipedal dinosaur was a swift, agile predator with a large brain that helped it to perform complex movements while chasing its prey.

Ancestors of birds

Deinonychus fossils were uncovered by Branum Brown in 1931 in Montana, USA, and J.H. Ostrom described and named *Deinonychus* in 1969. This was one of the important discoveries of the 20th century. It exploded the myth that dinosaurs were small-brained and dumb animals. The large-sized brain of the dinosaur was also responsible for its good sensory organ system. It also gave rise to the thought of dinosaurs being warm-blooded like birds and mammals.

Facts

- Velociraptor, Utahraptor and Oviraptor are some of the family members of Deinonychus.
- Like birds, Deinonychus had a wrist that could flex sideways.

Bird-like dinosaur

Deinonychus and its cousin *Dromaeosaurus* shared many similarities with the ancient *Archaeopteryx* and are believed to be the closest relative of this bird. In fact, *Archaeopteryx* is thought to be the closest link between birds and dinosaurs. This bird-like *Deinonychus* and *Archaeopteryx* both had long arms and hands. *Deinonychus* had a special claw that was bent upwards and almost seemed perpendicular to the feet. The name *Deinonychus* itself means 'terrible claw' as the dinosaur was named after its 12-cm long killing claw.

Who discovered the first Deinonychus fossil?

▼ *Deinonychus*

Dilophosaurus

Dilophosaurus was a lizard-hipped theropod. It lived about 200–190 million years ago (early Jurassic Period). It belonged to the family of Ceratosaurs and was a fierce predator and was thus nicknamed the 'terror of the early Jurassic'.

Head ornamentation

Dilophosaurus had a pair of thin bony crests on its head. These iridescent crests were semicircular in shape. It is for its head crest that this dinosaur was named *Dilophosaurus*, meaning 'double-crested lizard'. According to some paleontologists, the head ornamentation of this dinosaur was too fragile to be used as a weapon. Hence, *Dilophosaurus* may have used it for display purposes or for attracting mates.

What did it look like?

Dilophosaurus was almost the size of a modern-day polar bear. It was 6 m long from nose to tail, 1.5 m tall and weighed up to 453 kg. Its forelimbs were longer and had three fingers that were adorned with sharp, curved claws. *Dilophosaurus* also had lean hind limbs with four toes that helped it to run fast. It used its stiff tail for balancing its body and for making quick turns.

Facts

- Dilophosaurus was a nimble dinosaur. It could run at a speed of 45 km per hour.
- A kink in the upper jaw of Dilophosaurus is similar to the one modern crocodiles have.

Diet

Dilophosaurus used its piercing curved claws for attacking and killing preys. Although it had long knife-like teeth, its loose jawbones made it difficult for *Dilophosaurus* to stab its prey. Instead, its teeth were perfect for plucking flesh from the already dead animals.

What does the name Dilophosaurus mean?

▲ *Dilophosaurus*

Baryonyx

Baryonyx lived about 125 million years ago (early Cretaceous Period). This dinosaur was a lookalike of crocodiles. It belonged to the family of giant meat-eating theropods, which were much more powerful and intelligent than T. rex and *Gigantosaurus*.

Teeth and claws

Baryonyx's long snout was filled with 96 sharp and serrated teeth. Its lower jaw had 64 teeth and the upper jaw had 32 teeth that were perfect for catching fish. *Baryonyx* had twice as many teeth as any other carnivorous dinosaur. It was also known as 'heavy claw' for its long, curved claws. Each claw was about 31 cm long. It also prowled around rivers or lakes in order to catch fish. *Baryonyx* used its claws to catch slippery fish just like the modern-day grizzly bears. It was one of the piscivorous dinosaurs.

What did it look like?

Baryonyx was about 10 m long, 2.5 m tall and weighed about 2000 kg. It had a narrow snout filled with knife-like teeth, a short but straight neck and a long tail. It also had a small crest on its snout. Its nostrils were also placed at the back of its snout. Unlike all theropods, its forelimbs were also larger. It also had three fingers on its forelimbs and a large claw. *Baryonyx* was agile and could run really fast on its muscular hind limbs.

Facts

- Baryonyx belonged to the group of dinosaurs called Tetanuran as it was very different from other theropods. Some of the other Tetanuran were Allosaurus, Compsognathus, Coelurosauria, Velociraptor, and T. rex.

Baryonyx discovery

Baryonyx was the first meat-eating dinosaur to be unearthed in Britain. In 1983 its first fossil was discovered from a clay pit in Surrey, England, by paleontologist William Walker. British paleontologists Angela C. Milner and Alan J. Charig named the fossil '*Baryonyx walkeri*' after its discoverer. The *Baryonyx* fossil is now at display at the Natural History Museum in London.

> When was the *Baryonyx* fossil first discovered?

Baryonyx ▸

Extinction of Dinosaurs

All dinosaurs became extinct by the end of the Age of Reptiles about 65 million years ago (late Cretaceous Period) in a mass extinction. Many other animals such as plesiosaurs, mososaurs and ichthyosaurs along with pterosaurs and ammonite cephalopods, which were on earth for about 325 million years, also died out. What caused this great extinction is still a mystery which has given rise to many theories.

Climate change

Volcanic eruptions, continental drift and the rise in sea levels caused several climatic changes in the earth's atmosphere. The clouds of smoke and gases from the extremely massive extraterrestrial or volcanic activities may have covered the atmosphere and blocked the sun's rays from reaching the planet. This could have led to a sudden decrease in temperature which the dinosaurs could not bear and, hence, died out.

Extraterrestrial impact

The earth was hit by a huge asteroid or meteorite perhaps miles in diameter. This collision formed a thick layer of dust in the upper atmosphere, darkening the planet. Forest fires triggered by the collision might have added smoke to the sky. This theory has been proved by the presence of the iridium metal all over the earth, both on land and in oceans. Iridium is rarely found on earth's surface but is found in great abundance in meteorites. So scientists believe that the presence of iridium on earth is because of an extraterrestrial impact that killed dinosaurs.

Facts

- A giant meteorite called 'Chicxulub', about 180 km in diameter, hit the Yucatán Peninsula about 65 million years ago. It was believed to have caused the extinction of dinosaurs.
- During the mass extinction of dinosaurs, many families of brachiopods and sea sponges also disappeared.

When did the Age of Reptiles end?

Volcanic activities

The rise in volcanic activity on earth because of continental drift or after the extraterrestrial impact could have also resulted in the extinction of dinosaurs. The earth's core is rich in iridium and is a source of magma that is churned out in large amounts during volcanic eruptions. The enormous volcanic activities around the world would have spread iridium all over the earth. The evidence of large volcanic eruptions around India dates back to about 65 million years ago.

43

Glossary

Abundance: a large quantity of something

Angiosperm: a flowering plant

Ancient: belonging to the very distance past

Atmosphere: the blanket of gases surrounding the earth or any other planet

Climate: the type of weather that a particular region has over a long period

Collision: an act when two objects crash into each other

Colossal: very large

Continental drift: the movement of continents that led to their relocation

Decay: to rot

Depth perception: the ability to see things very clearly and to determine the distance between objects

Embryo: a baby developing inside an egg

Enormous: huge or very large

Extinction: the state of being completely wiped out

Extraterrestrial: related to things of outer space

Feeble: very weak

Fern: a plant that doesn't bear flowers and has feather-like leaves

Ferocious: extremely fierce

Geological timescale: the time period that involves the physical formation and development of the earth

Gigantic: very huge

Incubate: to sit on eggs for hatching

Iridescent: something that shows many colours that seem to change when seen from different angles

Iridium: a precious metal

Meteorite: a piece of rock from outer space that lands on a planet with a big collision

Mineral: a natural substance inside the earth's surface

Neural spine: the spinous process of a vertebra

Nimble: able to move quickly and with ease

Ornamentation: decoration to make something more beautiful

Pelvic bone: a bone that supports the lower part of our body and is connected to the bones of legs

Predator: an animal that hunts other animals for food

Prey: an animal that is hunted by other animals for food

Puny: small and weak

Rock strata: layers of rock

Scavenger: an animal that feeds on already dead and decaying animals

Sensory organ system: a set of organs that help in sensing surroundings

Stocky: bulky or heavyweight

Terrestrial: related to land

Vertebrae: small bones that make up the backbone

Answers

Page No. 9	Mesozoic Era
Page No. 11	Yes
Page No. 13	Paleontology
Page No. 14	Harry Seeley
Page No. 17	Cretaceous Period
Page No. 19	1963
Page No. 21	France
Page No. 23	Tyrant lizard king
Page No. 25	Spiny lizard
Page No. 27	Bird
Page No. 29	Roof lizard
Page No. 30	1877
Page No. 33	Jurassic Period
Page No. 35	1922, in Gobi Desert, Mongolia
Page No. 37	Branum Brown
Page No. 39	Double-crested lizard
Page No. 41	1983
Page No. 43	65 million years ago

BIRDS

Introduction

Birds and their extraordinary abilities have fascinated humans since time immemorial. They are creatures that have been endowed with wings and the ability to fly in the sky. Better known as the masters of the sky, birds are the only feathered creatures in the world. Their light-weight skeletal structures help them to take off into the air with ease. Their air mobility, bright plumage and unusual beaks have astounded everyone. Birds are found in the air, on land and in water.

While some birds spend their entire lives in the air traversing the world, some of them fly only if threatened and the others can't fly at all. There are about 9,000 bird species present on Earth. Different birds have different habits and characteristics. They range from tiny hummingbirds to huge eagles.

Evolution of Birds

Insects were the first creatures on Earth that took to the air. Later, animals with backbones also developed an alternative means of locomotion and became capable of flight. These animals are better known as birds. Their aerial existence can be traced back to about 190 million years ago during the Jurassic Age. Birds are believed to have evolved either from theropod dinosaurs (hollow bones, three toes and claws on each limb) or thecodont reptiles (teeth in bony sockets).

Archaeopteryx

A strange fossil of a bird-like creature was found in Germany in 1861. This specimen not only had teeth but also had evidence of feathers impressed upon the stones. It resembled both a bird and a reptile with a fused collarbone and bird-like feet. Scientists concluded that this was the oldest bird fossil, and it was named Archaeopteryx, meaning 'ancient wings'.

Origin of flight

Flight may have originated as a development in arboreal reptiles or dinosaurs that used to glide between trees at great heights. However, another theory says that birds needed to feed on insects and, thus, found a way of raising themselves from the ground. The leaping activity among the dinosaurs could have led to the development of wings to ensure a smooth landing.

Dinosaurs and birds

It is believed that dinosaurs are the closest relatives of birds. A dinosaur fossil with wings found in China strengthened the theory that birds might have evolved from dinosaurs. Their skeletal features resembled those of birds. Pterosaurs, or flying dinosaurs, also ruled the skies during the Jurassic Age. However, their wings were shaped more like those of bats than birds.

Facts

- It is believed that feathers originated from reptilian scales.
- Feathers originated long before the evolution of flight. They were initially meant for insulation purposes.

Name the oldest known bird.

Feathers

Birds are the only species of animals in the world that have feathers. The entire body of a bird, apart from the beak, legs and feet, is covered with feathers. Feathers are made up of a protein called keratin, which is also found in human hair and nails. There are mainly three purposes of feathers in birds.

Warmth

Birds have small and soft down feathers attached to their skin to keep them warm. Feathers provide a barrier that retains warm air close to the birds' body. These wispy down feathers help maintain their body temperature typically between 41 and 43.5°C.

Flight feathers

Flight feathers help birds during flight and enable them to soar in the sky. They are attached to the bone through ligaments. The outer flight feathers, also known as primaries, are the largest and strongest of all flight feathers. The inner flight feathers, also called secondaries, are found between the bird's body and the primaries.

Decorative feathers

The body or plume feathers are usually for decorative purposes. These contour feathers also help in camouflage and attract birds of the opposite sex. A peacock has a very beautiful train of feathers, which it opens out to deter rivals and attract mates. This display is one of the most remarkable sights associated with birds.

Moulting and bathing

Birds often keep their feathers in good condition by moulting and bathing. In the process of moulting, birds shed their old feathers and grow a new plumage, which helps them in getting rid of parasites and old and weak feathers. Birds often bathe in rainwater or splash themselves in pools of water to remove dirt and debris from their feathers.

Facts

- Some hummingbirds and sunbirds have feathers that sparkle at night, creating an iridescent effect.
- A swan may have as many as 25,000 feathers.

What are feathers made of?

Bird Beaks and Feeding

Birds have the most unusual mouth that does not have any lips or teeth. Their beak helps them in eating, catching prey and feeding the young. Their beak is made of a lightweight bone known as horn. Beaks vary widely in shape, size and colour depending on the feeding habits of birds. While some birds are plant-eaters, others are predators or scavengers.

Crows

Crows are omnivorous and eat a wide variety of things, including plants, insects, spiders, snails, fish, eggs, nuts, fruits and vegetables. They have all-purpose heavy beaks that help them in their diverse feeding habits.

Woodpeckers

Woodpeckers have straight and strong chisel-like beaks, which are meant for pecking. They use their pointed bill to drill homes in dead wood and to search for food.

Pelicans

Pelicans are waterbirds that mainly feed on fish. These birds have a large fleshy pouch in place of their lower mandibles, which is used to scoop up fish from the water.

Crossbills

Crossbills have a very unusual bills that cross at the tip. The shape of their bills allows these birds to open up pine cones and remove the seeds.

> Name the bird that has a fleshy pouch in place of its lower mandible.

Seed-eating birds

Some songbirds, such as finches and buntings, have a strong conical beak for crushing hard seeds and removing their outer covering.

Flamingos

Flamingos have unique beaks (bills) that help them to feed with their head upside down. They use their beaks to filter food from shallow waters.

Ducks

Ducks, such as spoonbills and waders, have a broad bill with flattened tip. They use their spatulate bills to skim for food in shallow waters.

Insect-eating birds

Insect-eating birds, such as flycatchers, warblers and thrushes, have special beaks adapted for feeding on insects. Their bills are broad and slightly hooked, with specialized bristles.

Raptors

Birds of prey, such as eagles, owls, hawks and falcons, have hooked beaks that help them tear the flesh of their prey.

Facts
- The wrybill is the only bird with a beak that curves to the right.
- Birds have a sharp, blade-like tongue that has bones inside it.

Mating

Birds often search for a mate during the breeding season. Some birds pair up only fleetingly, some birds pair up for the whole breeding season and some species pair for life. Birds use a variety of tactics to find mates.

Bird songs

Many birds sing during the breeding season, not only to attract mates but also to establish their territory. In some cases, both cocks and hens sing a beautiful duet during the mating season. Pairs of Japanese cranes perform a spectacular dance by leaping into the air, raising their wings and making trumpet calls.

Bright plumage

Males often moult before the breeding season to display their brightly coloured plumage to the females. Their bright-coloured feathers and wings help them to attract females. Females, on the other hand, are usually dull, which helps them to camouflage while caring for the young.

Which bird displays a beautiful dance during the mating season?

Breeding behaviour

Some groups of birds, such as cocks-of-the-rock and Birds of Paradise, assemble in communal display areas known as leks, where males display themselves and the females select a mate. Some male birds, such as the satin bowerbird and the red bishop beaver bird, make beautiful nests and bowers, which are inspected by the females. These nests are decorated with grass, twigs, flowers, etc.

Facts

- Bird calls can travel up to a distance of 5 km in case of some species, such as bellbirds and bitterns, that sing particularly penetrating songs.
- Male ruffs compete with each other in displays to attract female partners.

Nests

Birds construct their own homes known as nests, where they lay eggs and incubate them. Some birds use tree holes for nesting, while others build nests on tree branches and rocks. Nests are built from all kinds of vegetation that are easily available. Some artificial materials, such as plastic wrappers, have also been found in birds' nests. The simplest nests are cup-shaped with a soft lining of feathers inside.

Biggest nest

One of the biggest nests is made by the bald eagle in a tall tree or on rocks. This nest is made up of sticks, and can be as big as 2.5 m across and 3.5 m deep. It is big enough to contain several people.

Weaved nests

A male weaver bird weaves and knots pieces of grass and stems to construct a long nest that hangs from the branch of a tree. The nest has a roof and a long narrow opening. It provides a safe shelter for the eggs.

Which bird creates the biggest nest?

Mud nests

Swallows scoop up muddy waters from the surface of a pond, mould the wet mud into the desired shape and then allow it to dry and harden like cement.

Cage nests

A male hornbill walls up his female mate and her eggs in a tree hole. It plasters the nest hole with mud leaving only a small opening to transfer food. This is done to protect the eggs from lizards and snakes. The female breaks the barrier only when the chicks are grown up.

Facts

- A cave swiftlet makes its nest from its own saliva, spit, feathers and grass.
- Woodpeckers create nesting chambers in tree holes by using their powerful bills.

Temperature-controlled mounds

The mallee fowl from Australia creates a natural incubator for its young ones by building a natural mound made of plants covered with sand. This mound emits warmth because of the decaying vegetation. The male keeps checking the temperature of the mound with its beak.

Young Ones

All birds reproduce by laying eggs, which have a hard calcareous covering. The colour and the number of eggs laid at a time vary depending on the nesting site. Birds that make open, cup-shaped nests often lay pale-coloured or mottled eggs. The colour of eggs helps to camouflage them and protects them from predators.

Incubation

Most birds incubate their eggs to keep them warm so that the chicks can grow well inside. Usually, the female bird takes up the responsibility of incubating, but in ostriches, the male bird incubates and takes care of the chick. Male and female pigeons and doves share their incubation duties.

Rearing

A parent bird has to take care of its large brood of young ones by supplying them with adequate food. Young birds often leave their nests about 12 to 30 days after hatching. Most young birds are not able to fly when they leave their nest since their flight feathers are not developed.

Hatching

A chick uses its beak to cut the inner membrane of the egg to breathe air. After 48 hours, it breaks the eggshell to emerge completely. The offspring of parrots and finches are completely blind, vulnerable and dependent on their parents when they hatch. However, the chicks of game birds, such as waterfowl, pheasants and waders, can see, run around and feed themselves as soon as they hatch.

Facts

- The cuckoo, a parasitic bird, lays its eggs in some other bird's nest while the host bird is not watching.
- Seabirds, such as the guillemot, lay a more pointed egg so that it does not tumble and fall off rocky cliffs.

Young birds often leave their nests in about _____ after hatching.

Migration

Some species of birds do not live in a particular place all around the year. They take seasonal journeys along specific routes across the world. Such birds are known as migratory and their journeys are called migrations. With their unique flying ability, birds fly north into temperate latitudes in the spring and return to the south at the end of the summer.

Why do birds migrate?

Birds migrate to seek shelter, to find safe areas, to rear their young and also to find areas where food is plentiful. Seasonal changes and changes in vegetation resulting in the scarcity of food in a particular area force birds to look for different settlement. Birds often eat large quantities of food before starting to store energy while flying long distances.

Migratory routes

The migratory routes that birds follow every year are well-defined. Land birds prefer taking coastal routes rather than flying over a large expanse of ocean. Studies have shown that birds navigate themselves using sunlight, the position of stars and familiar landmarks. Migrating birds fly at great speeds and high altitudes. Geese have been spotted crossing the Himalayas at a height of 7,200 m.

Arctic tern

Arctic tern make the longest migration journeys of all animals. They breed in the Arctic in the summer and fly to Antarctica before returning in the winter. They cover distances of more than 30,000 km on their journey around the world. An Arctic tern can live to be more than 30 years, which means that it may fly around the world 20 times during its lifetime.

Facts

- Birds often fly in groups while covering large distances.
- Scientists have identified migratory habits of birds by placing a band around their legs, which helps in identifying individual birds.

Which bird has the longest migration journey of all animals?

Flightless Birds

Flightless birds have feathers and wings but don't possess the ability to fly. They include some of the largest birds in the world such as ostriches, penguins, rheas and emus. Flightless birds depend on other means of locomotion, such as running or swimming, to catch prey in their natural environment. These birds usually have small wings and a heavy body.

Emus

These Australian giants are the second tallest birds in the world. They have tiny wings with coarse and floppy feathers. Found in the desert areas of Australia, the emus can travel long distances in search of grass, seeds and insects to eat.

Cassowaries

Cassowaries are found in the tropical rainforests of Australia and New Guinea. These tall birds have long, razor-sharp claws, which they use to defend themselves from hunters. Cassowaries also have a large, bony structure on their head, which is called casque.

Ostriches

Ostriches are the tallest birds and also the world's fastest birds on the ground. They have long, powerful legs and can run up to 50 km per hour. A long neck and keen eyesight enables them to see enemies from afar. Found in Africa, these flightless birds can grow up to 2.7 m and can weigh up to 158 kg. An ostrich has just two toes on each foot.

Kiwis

These little birds from New Zealand live in swamps and grasslands. Kiwis are nocturnal birds. They have a small body and short legs and cannot run fast. They are named after their unusual call, which is a high-pitched whistle. Kiwis have a good sense of smell. They use their nostrils located at the end of their beak to smell insects and worms on the ground.

Facts

- Ostrich eggs are the largest of all bird eggs. One egg weighs around 1.5 kg.
- The dodo, a large flightless bird from the Mauritius Islands in the Indian Ocean, has gone extinct because of the destruction of its natural habitat.

Name the fastest bird on land.

Game Birds

Game birds are a terrestrial group of birds that have short round bodies and smaller wings. These birds cannot fly long distances but are good runners. Game birds are often domesticated or hunted by humans for food and other uses. There are about 260 different species in this group, including pheasants, quails, chickens, ducks, geese, turkeys and more.

Pheasants

Pheasants are a group of birds that belong to the same family as peacocks. They are characterized by small wattled heads and long tails. A male pheasant is called a rooster, while a female pheasant is called a hen. A typical rooster breeds a group of three to seven hens.

Facts

- The crested argus pheasant has the longest tail of all birds. It can grow up to 1.73 m in length.
- Many quail chicks are relatively mature and mobile from the moment of hatching, so they can leave the nest with their parents.

Evolution

As a result of the domestication and interbreeding of game birds for food, several new breeds of farm birds evolved. Chicken, the most common farm bird, is believed to have descended from the red jungle fowl. Mallards are considered to be the ancestors of the domestic breeds of ducks. Significant changes took place in these birds over the years, which also hampered their ability to fly.

Turkeys

Turkeys are large birds that have a flap of skin in their throat region. This outgrowth of skin can turn red when the turkey is upset or during courtship. They are largely hunted and considered a delicacy, especially during the Christmas season.

A male pheasant is called a _____.

Seabirds

Many birds live near the vast oceans of the world and feed on the many ocean resources. These birds are powerful fliers and can soar high above the seas in search of fish, squid or krill. These birds can not only swim well but also often dive in water often to catch prey. Seabirds have a special salt-excreting gland in the nasal area that allows them to drink seawater without getting dehydrated.

Cormorants

Cormorants catch fish by diving and chasing them underwater. These birds can stay submerged for quite some time. These birds are mostly found in large colonies in a wide variety of sites. They are often seen drying out their feathers in the sun after a dive. Oil spillage and hunting by humans pose a great threat to these birds.

> What is the wingspan of a wandering albatross?

Gannets

Gannets are large seabirds that are often found in huge breeding colonies. These birds gather in the spring to nest together on rocks beside the sea. Gannets can dive underwater to catch fish. Their streamlined shape enables them to swim with ease.

Frigate bird

Frigate birds are attractive aerial hunters that scoop up flying fish and squid from the surface of the water. These opportunistic feeders also chase other seabirds and force them to drop their prey. These birds breed in colonies on remote islands.

Albatrosses

Albatrosses are large seabirds that remain airborne for much of their lives with the help of their long, slender wings. A wandering albatross has the largest wingspan than any other bird, measuring up to 3.4 m.

Facts

- Gannets are gliding birds that have large wings, which catch currents and carry them into the air.
- Some albatross species are heavily hunted for their feathers that are used to make hats for women.

Swimming Birds

Although most birds are adapted to flying in the air, some birds have developed alternative means of locomotion. Some birds, such as penguins, ducks, geese and swans, are excellent swimmers that plunge into water in search of food. Aquatic birds have special characteristics, such as webbed feet, waterproof feathers, a streamlined body and powerful wings.

Flightless swimmers

Penguins found in the Antarctic region are the best swimmers in the bird world. They are extremely well adapted to live in their natural environment and spend most of their time in the icy cold waters of the Antarctic. Penguins have sleek torpedo-shaped bodies that allow them to swim fast underwater. Their wings or flippers help them to steer very effectively as they pursue fish and krill in the water. Penguins are the deepest divers and can hold their breath for up to 27 minutes in water.

Surface paddlers

This group includes ducks, geese and swans. These birds have webbed feet, which they use as paddles to swim on the surface of the water. Swans are long-necked, graceful birds that glide on water. These birds mainly feed on water plants and algae growing in a pond by plunging their necks inside the water.

> Name two swimming birds.

Surface divers

Some birds can float on water as well as dive underwater such as grebes, coots, auks, auklets, dovekies, guillemots and petrels. Grebes have flattened, lobed toes that help in swimming and diving. They are known to float lower than ducks and have the habit of submerging themselves completely in water at the approach of any danger. This practice has given them the name, hell-diver, the auk family consists of excellent divers who use their wings for propulsion in water.

Facts

- On land, penguins walk with a waddle and often slide on the snow on their bellies.
- A coot has lobed feet that enable it to run on the surface of water for a take-off into the air.

Birds of Prey

Birds of prey are carnivores that use their feet instead of their beak to catch prey. They have sharp talons, which help them to catch their prey while flying, diving or gliding. Birds of prey have large eyes as compared to their head and a keen vision. There are about 500 species of birds of prey that include eagles, falcons, hawks, kites, vultures and owls.

Eagles

Eagles are large birds with hooked beaks and strong claws, which they use to grab their prey. Most eagles are known to catch prey without landing. They seize the prey and kill it with their strong talons. Eagles feed on mammals such as hares and rabbits. Some golden eagles catch tortoises and then drop them from a height to a rock outcrop to break open the shell.

Falcons

Falcons have tapered, pointed wings built to provide them speed and agility. Most falcons do not build a nest and stay in the abandoned nests of other birds. The peregrine falcon is one of the fastest birds with a diving speed of up to 321 km per hour. It hunts other birds in the air such as pigeons and doves. It often perches on tall buildings, trees or poles.

Vultures

Vultures have adapted to feed on dead animals. They have a strong sense of smell, which helps them to eat only fresh carcasses and reject decomposing meat. Vultures regurgitate food from their crops for their young instead of carrying prey to the nest. The Andean condor is one of the largest flying birds. It resides in caves or on ledges in a cliff face.

Name two birds of prey.

Facts

- Peregrine falcons are one of the most common birds that are found in every continent except Antarctica.
- The osprey is a seabird that feeds largely on fish. There is only one species of osprey that can be found in every continent.

Forest Birds

Rainforests are home to some of the most spectacular species of birds. Many of these birds are brightly coloured, but their vibrant plumage is concealed in the dark, shadowy environment. Forest birds spend most of their time in trees and feed on fruits.

Quetzals

Quetzals are beautiful birds with a red belly and iridescent green head, back, chest and wings. During the mating season, male quetzals grow magnificent twin tail feathers that form an amazing train up to a length of 1 m. Quetzals were considered sacred by the Mayan and Aztec people. This bird is the national bird of Guatemala.

Toucans

Toucans found in the rainforests of South America have large, lightweight and colourful beaks that assist them in reaching fruits at the end of the branches, which would otherwise be inaccessible. Toucans have two claws in the front and two claws at the back that help them to hold on to the tree branches.

Toucans eat fruits. True/False?

Birds of Paradise

Birds of Paradise are beautifully coloured birds found in the rainforests of Southeast Asia, mainly in the jungles of Indonesia and New Guinea. These birds are best known for their striking colours, attractive plumage, and dramatic courtship rituals. Males have amazingly elongated feathers, which are known as wires or streamers. Some species have distinctive ornaments such as breast shields, plumes or head fans. During the mating season, they display elaborate dances, poses and other rituals.

Facts

- The scarlet macaw is one of the largest parrots in the world.
- The enormous bills of toucans are mostly filled with air. They have little practical purpose and are mainly meant to help in feeding.

Perching Birds

Perching birds and songbirds are the most common birds in the world. There are more than 5,000 species of perching birds. Their highly-developed voice organ, known as the syrinx, allows them to sing and produce musical notes. Perching birds have three toes pointing forward and one toe pointing backwards, which is ideal for holding onto branches.

Swallows

Swallows are small perching birds that are adept in hunting and feeding on the wing by catching insects in mid-air. They have long and forked tails. Barn swallows initially made their nests in caves, but now they nest on the top of buildings or cliffs. Young swallows eat around 850 insects per day, which are brought to them by their parents.

Nightingales

Synonymous with melody, these small morning birds can often be heard singing at dawn. Their loud songs, which include whistles, trills and gurgles can also be heard at night. These timid and romantic birds have been an inspiration for poets throughout the ages.

> Name the bird which has been an inspiration for poets.

Crows

Unlike thrushes and nightingales, crows have a harsh voice and are often found communicating in shrill sounds. Crows are highly adaptable to diverse environments and are also found in cities and suburban areas.

Facts

- The colour of a nightingale's egg is deep olive. It usually lays five to six eggs at a time.
- A magpie is a type of crow that steals the eggs of other birds from their nests.

Mockingbirds

Mockingbirds are songbirds that are famous for their habit of imitating other bird songs and sounds and repeating them loudly over and over again. These birds can also mimic sounds of amphibians, cars, sirens and insects. The song of a mocking bird is a medley of the calls of other birds.

Freshwater Birds

Many birds, such as ducks, geese, flamingos and herons are found by lakes, ponds and rivers. These birds are drawn to such freshwater habitats because of the food and nesting opportunities. They have special adaptations, such as webbed feet and special beaks, that help them live on the banks of freshwater bodies.

Storks and cranes

Storks and cranes are tall wading birds with long legs and strong bills. These birds stand upright in the water and catch fish, amphibians, reptiles and insects. These birds are found in open grasslands and freshwater marshes.

Kingfishers

As the name suggests, kingfishers are brightly coloured birds that mainly feed on fish. These birds stay perched motionless above the water in search of a potential catch. They have a large head, a long bill and delicate feet that help them dive into water to catch fish. They often slam their fish against a tree before swallowing them whole.

Flamingos

Flamingos are tall, pinkish birds that are found in warm regions. Their colonies are usually seen near shallow lakes and lagoons. Their pinkish colour is due to the presence of carotene in the food they eat. They have long, slender legs and beaks that are covered with hair-like bristles. Often standing on one leg, they hold their beaks upside down to draw water into their mouths. The bristles act as a filter and trap water, shrimps, snails and algae in their mouth.

Name two freshwater birds.

Facts
- The eyes of a flamingo are larger than its brain.
- It is possible for a family of kingfishers to eat up to 100 fish a day.

Nocturnal Birds

Some birds, such as owls and nighthawks, are active at night. These birds hunt at night, and some even migrate during nightfall. They are some of the mysterious and fascinating members of the bird kingdom.

Nightjars

Nightjars are a strictly nocturnal group of birds that are most active at dawn and dusk. They spend their nights hunting for moths, beetles and other insects. With a perfectly camouflaged plumage, they rest during the day among leaf litter on the ground. Male nightjars are known to produce a loud 'churring' call.

Facts

- Owls have asymmetrical ears on their head, usually at different heights, which give them superior hearing power during hunting.
- Many small birds, including warblers and flycatchers, feed in the daytime and migrate at night at the cost of their sleep.

Frogmouths

Frogmouths are closely related to owls and nightjars. These nocturnal birds have a large and wide frog-like mouth to capture insects. Their bills are large, horn-like and triangular. During the day, these birds usually rest on tree branches. While hunting, frogmouths stay very quiet and capture insects and spiders in their enormous mouth. The feathers around their mouth resemble whiskers and help trap a large prey inside the mouth.

Owls

Owls are one of the most common nocturnal birds of prey. There are more than 200 species of owls, including barn owls and true owls. Barn owls have heart-shaped heads and are mostly medium-sized. Owls have forward-facing eyes that are largely fixed in the sockets. Owls have an astonishing ability to rotate their head up to 270 degrees to see things behind them. They have amazing night vision, which enables them to hunt rodents, snakes and insects at night. At night time, they face less competition from the diurnal hunters. Owls produce a variety of sounds, including hoots, screeches, whistles and hisses. Owls have special feathers in their wings that help them to fly without making any sound.

Name a nocturnal bird.

Hummingbirds

Hummingbirds are the tiniest species of birds that mainly hover around flowers and drink nectar with their long needle-like bills. They have beautifully coloured plumage and some of them also have iridescent feathers that glow in the dark. They are mainly flower feeders and help in the fertilization of flowers by spreading pollen grains.

Hovering hummingbirds

Hummingbirds get their name from the low humming or buzzing sound produced by the fast flapping of their wings. They beat their wings more frequently than any other bird. These birds can hover in front of a flower while drinking its nectar by beating their wings backwards and forward very quickly. Some hummingbirds flap their wings around 720 to 4,800 beats per minute. A hummingbird can rotate its wings in a circle. This makes them the only group of birds that can fly forward, backwards, up, down, sideways and hover in mid-air.

Facts
- A hummingbird's heart rate can reach up to 1,260 beats per minute.
- Hummingbirds can see ultraviolet light.

Bee hummingbirds

The bee hummingbird is the smallest bird and measures up to 5.7 cm long. This smallest living bird is mainly found in Cuba. Its nest is no longer than one inch in diameter and its eggs are the size of green peas.

Hungry hummingbirds

Hummingbirds have the highest metabolism rate among all birds. To support their high activity rate, they need a lot of food and can consume more nectar than their body weight. In their non-stop search for food, they visit hundreds of flowers daily. While sleeping or when food is scarce, hummingbirds can go into a hibernation-like state known as torpor to prevent themselves from starving. During this state, they slow down their metabolism rate and often appear to be dead.

Name the smallest living bird.

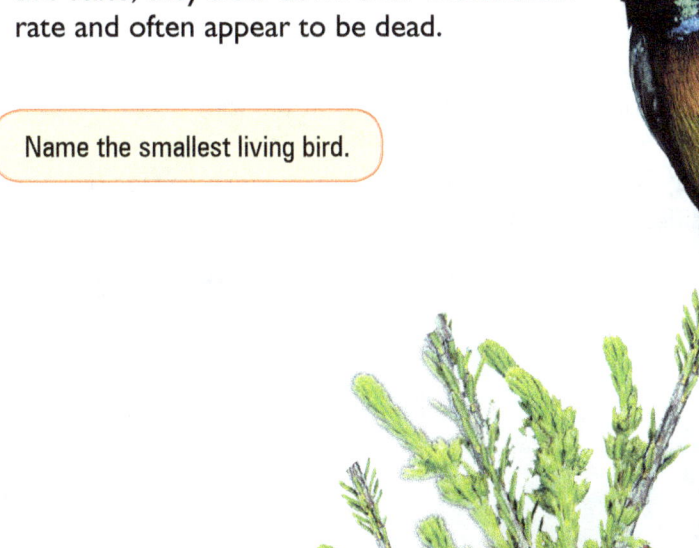

Intelligence

Birds are often thought to be brainless or dimwitted. However, studies have proved that some birds are quite smart. In comparison to their body size, birds have larger brains. Some birds can solve complex problems by insight and can also communicate meaningfully in a variety of ways.

Pigeons

Pigeons are known to distinguish between different paintings. They also have discriminating abilities. They are extremely good at navigation and can easily find their way back home. Homing pigeons were earlier used to deliver messages to different places.

Facts

- A study has proved that coots can count eggs.
- Hummingbirds have sharp brains and can teach other birds how to sing.

Which parrot has the intelligence of a small child?

Corvid family

Crows, ravens and jays are perhaps the most intelligent of all birds. These birds display extraordinary abilities that have astonished scientists. Some crows are known to crack nuts at traffic signals by waiting for the cars to pass over the nuts. They are also believed to have the capacity to create simple tools and use them. The Clark's nutcracker, a type of crow, is known for its sharp memory. It often buries seeds and can retrieve them from the ground even after months.

Parrots

Parrots are another group of intelligent birds that have the ability to mimic human speech. African grey parrots are believed to have the intelligence of a three- to four-year-old child. Scientists have proved that these parrots can remember a vocabulary of 100 words and frame meaningful sentences. Keas are another example of intelligent birds belonging to this group. They are capable of solving complex puzzles to reach food.

Glossary

Breeding: the process of mating and reproducing young ones

Calcareous: chalky

Camouflage: the ability of organisms to change their colour according to their surrounding environment

Carcass: the body of a dead animal

Decay: to rot

Decompose: to decay or rot gradually

Dehydrate: cause to lose a large amount of water

Delicacy: a special type of food

Delicate: very weak

Diurnal: during the day

Domesticate: to train an animal or a bird to keep as a pet or to farm it

Extinct: an organism that is dead and no longer exists

Fertilization: the process that begins the reproduction cycle in living beings

Fossil: remains of ancient plants and animals buried deep inside the Earth for millions of years

Grassland: a large piece of land where wild grass grows

Hibernation: a state of deep sleep in which an animal uses its accumulated fat to survive extreme weather conditions

Incubate: a bird sits on its eggs to keep them warm until the baby birds hatch from them

Iridescent: to show different colours that appear to change when seen from different angles

Jurassic Age: the period that began after the triassic period, in which dinosaurs flourished in large numbers

Locomotion: the ability to move around

Metabolism: the process by which energy and nutrients are extracted from food for the survival of living beings

Mottle: mark with spots

Navigate: to find the way or path

Parasite: an organism that lives on another organism for food and nutrition

Plentiful: in abundance or large quantity

Plumage: a bird's feathers

Pollen Grain: a dust-like powder present in flowers, which is carried by winds or bees to other flowers for reproduction

Predator: an organism that hunts other organisms for food

Prey: an organism that is hunted by a predator

Sacred: related to God or the divine

Scarcity: shortage

Scavenger: an organism that feeds on the dead remains of other organisms

Spectacular: very attractive or impressive

Swamp: a land near lakes, rivers or any other waterbody, which is partially covered with water and some vegetation

Synonymous: similar or closely related

Timid: shy or bashful

Answers

Page No. 51 Archaeopteryx

Page No. 53 Keratin

Page No. 54 Pelican

Page No. 57 Japanese crane

Page No. 58 Bald eagle

Page No. 61 12–30 days

Page No. 63 Arctic tern

Page No. 65 Ostrich

Page No. 67 Rooster

Page No. 68 3.4 m

Page No. 70 Ducks and penguins

Page No. 73 Peregrine falcon and Andean condor

Page No. 74 True

Page No. 76 Nightingale

Page No. 79 Storks and cranes

Page No. 81 Owl

Page No. 83 Bee hummingbird

Page No. 84 African grey parrot

www.ingramcontent.com/pod-product-compliance
Lightning Source LLC
Chambersburg PA
CBHW050657160426
43194CB00010B/1982